EXTREME MOTORSPORTS

Jeff Mapua

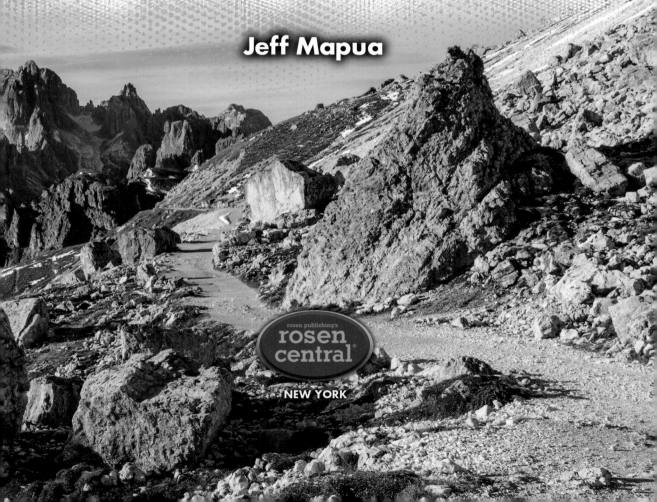

rosen publishing's
rosen
central

NEW YORK

Published in 2016 by The Rosen Publishing Group, Inc.
29 East 21st Street, New York, NY 10010

Library of Congress Cataloging-in-Publication Data

Mapua, Jeff.
Extreme motorsports/Jeff Mapua.—First Edition.
    pages cm.—((Sports to the Extreme))
Includes bibliographical references and index.
Audience: Grades 5–8.
ISBN 978-1-4994-3549-8 (Library bound) — ISBN 978-1-4994-3551-1 (Paperback) -- ISBN 978-1-4994-3552-8 (6-pack)
1. Motorsports—Juvenile literature. 2. Racing—Juvenile literature. 3. Speed—Juvenile literature. I. Title.
GV1019.2.M36 2015
796.7--dc23

2014044182

Manufactured in the United States of America

CONTENTS

INTRODUCTION

At an exotic locale, spectators gather to watch daredevil athletes fly through the air on powerful motorcycles. Seemingly impossible stunts like a double backflip are just another sight to behold at the latest stop on the Red Bull X-Fighters motocross tour. Elsewhere around the world, drivers in everything from go-karts to speedboats push their motors to their most extreme abilities.

Extreme motorsports are fast and dangerous, and they are not for the faint of heart. To be considered an extreme motorsport, competitors are put into dangerous situations that go beyond the risks of most sports.

Races may not be held on enclosed tracks, and stunts are not only encouraged, but can mean the difference between winning and a second-place finish. In some extreme motorsports, racers strap rockets to their cars to see how

4

Televised events like the X Games bring extreme motorsports like motocross flying into homes around the world.

fast they can possibly go. The physical limits are constantly pushed, and sometimes they can even be pushed too far.

In June 2013, the world-famous Le Mans event began with competitors ready for the high-speed endurance race. This twenty-four-hour car race is a test of mechanical engineering, driving ability, and stamina. But just ten minutes into the 2013 race, tragedy struck. In a spot on the race track where cars are speeding around at over 100 miles per hour (161 kilometers per hour), Danish driver Allan Simonse lost control of his car. His car began spinning and crashed into a barrier. He was taken to a nearby hospital where he was pronounced dead. Professional racer James Jakes was quoted as saying, "It's tough, but it's the world we live in."

Setting world records for being the fastest or for doing the most stunts is not without risks. But for those who love extreme motorsports, it is a risk worth taking.

CHAPTER ONE

EXTREME CAR RACING

When the automotive industry began in the late 1890s, with the invention of the horseless carriage, it would have been difficult to predict what drivers would be doing behind the wheel over a hundred years later. As automobile technology advanced over the years, cars could be pushed to new limits. Slowly cruising down a roadway is no longer enough for some drivers. Even the idea of keeping all four of the car's wheels firmly on the ground is in the rearview mirror for extreme drivers.

THE BEGINNING OF CAR RACING

Car racing had a long history in Europe before it came to America. The first trophy for an American automobile race was the 1904 Vanderbilt Cup, which took place on Long Island, New York. Stock car racing began as a competition between cars that had not been altered. But once tweaks to make the cars faster were discovered, they had unusual boosters just a few years later among bootleggers, when Prohibition made having a fast car a necessity.

Early cars like this Bluebird looked very different from the cars of today. Even the equipment that race car drivers use has evolved.

In 1920, the Eighth Amendment made it illegal to manufacture, sell, or transport alcohol. However, that did not stop whiskey distillers in the American South. They used cheap cars to transport their product and tweaked the cars so that they were faster than the law enforcement cars that chased them down but still looked just like all the other cars on the road. When a pair of illegal whiskey distillers challenged each other to see who had the faster transport car, racing these tweaked stock cars soon followed.

Races were held on secluded dirt roads, old horse tracks, and beaches such as Daytona in Florida. Spectators began demanding closed race tracks to let them view the entire race rather than just a small part. Businessmen soon came to their aid and capitalized on the new money-making opportunity.

After Prohibition ended in the 1930s, selling, making, and transporting alcohol was no longer illegal, but stock car racing continued. People continued to make improvements to race cars, which caused car racing to split off into different events—some with vehicles that sometimes looked like cars on the road, and some that bore little resemblance to the models found at a car dealership.

OFF-ROAD AND DESERT RACING

Even with the introduction of race tracks that eventually led to organized racing, off-road racing remained popular among drivers. Any kind of racing that occurs off of paved roads and on surfaces such as dirt or sand is considered off-road. Drivers must compete not only against one another, but against the race course, too.

TYPES OF CARS

Normal street cars would not be great off-road vehicles. In order for the car to survive the difficult conditions of an off-road or desert event, cars must be heavily modified. In addition to changes to the engines to make them more powerful, mechanics may add or take away parts to improve the car's performance. This can even include removing windows, doors, and panels of the car's body.

Many off-road cars are built to be more rugged and with less concern for aerodynamics. The suspension system of a car helps reduce the bumpiness of the ride. Off-road cars must have great suspension systems, which are made up of shock absorbers, springs, and bars located on the underside of the car.

Tires are usually large in order to maneuver over uneven and rocky tracks. Many cars have roll cages, which a driver is strapped into as protection from injury caused by heavy bumps and occasional rolling. Engines are built to maximize speed without overheating. It is just as important for the engine to be reliable as it is for it to be powerful.

TYPES OF RACES

Desert racing is one type of off-road racing. In the 1920s, Californians began racing in the desert. From 1964 to 1989, the most popular desert race had drivers start in Barstow, California, and speed toward the finish line in Las Vegas, Nevada. Some desert races consist of two loops around a course of up to 40 miles (64 km). A Hare and Hound race is a two-lap event around a course. When the race begins, the car in front becomes the hare, and all other cars are the hound chasing the hare. A Hare Scramble is similar to the Hare and Hound, only it is held in an open course rather than a track.

Another type of race is called a rally. An off-road rally is called a rally raid. These are held over several days, and drivers must race from one point to another each day. This is called point-to-point racing. One of the most popular rally raids is the Dakar Rally (also called the Dakar or the Paris-Dakar Rally), which was originally held in North Africa. Since 2009, it has been held in South America due to security problems. This race is held over many days and crosses numerous countries. Many consider it the toughest race in the world.

The Baja 1000 is a famous off-road race held in the Baja California Peninsula in

Mexico. The name is misleading as the race is not always 1,000 miles (1,609 km) and is made up of a group of smaller races. There are loop and point-to-point races. Cars, motorcycles, and trucks race in the Baja 1000.

A car from the 2014 Bull Run in South Africa races through the desert. In this race, new cars are not used. Drivers must use vehicles that are at least thirty years old.

DRAG RACING

In the 1930s, people built stripped-down versions of cars and raced them on dirt tracks and city streets. These cars were called hot rods, and the community of people who enjoyed this type of racing was considered antisocial and a public nuisance. By holding events in deserts and dry lakes, the racers known as hot rodders tested their courage and engineering skills by reaching new speeds.

TYPES OF CARS

Originally, early Ford cars were popular drag racers, including the Model T, the Deuce, and other roadsters. Over time, car designs evolved as technology improved and styles changed. By the 1960s, top machines could reach 220 miles per hour (354 km/h) in only seven seconds. Even today, the top speed of the average car only reaches 150 miles per hour (241 km/h).

TYPES OF RACES

Today, there are two main types of drag races. The most competitive is called heads-up racing. The rules are simple: two cars start at the same point then race each other to a finish line. The first one there wins. The second type of race is called bracket racing. This style is more complex, but the basic rules have two racers predicting how fast they will finish the race. They then begin at different times in order for the racers to finish at the same time and are penalized if they go faster than their guess.

ENDURANCE RACING

In 1909, a man named Erwin Baker rode a motorcycle across the United States. As a way to promote their cars, automobile

JATO ROCKET CARS

A famous urban legend describes how a driver strapped a jet-assisted takeoff booster, or JATO, to a car. The small cylinder filled with fuel was ignited, and the car supposedly hit speeds around 350 miles per hour (563 km/h), became airborne, and hit the side of a mountain at 125 feet (38 meters) off the ground. Although this tall tale has been proven to be false, the JATO rocket car does exist.

A German by the name of Fritz van Opel attached twenty-four small rockets to his car in 1928 and reached a speed of 143 miles per hour (230 km/h). In 1970, the rocket-powered car Blue Flame set a land-speed record of 630 miles per hour (1,014 km/h). Jet-powered cars were popular in drag races until a surge of fatal accidents in the 1970s slowed their usage.

A famous, and true, story of a JATO car occurred in 1946 when professional racer Andy Granatelli fit military-surplus JATO rockets onto a race car. After a successful test and a few mechanical tweaks, Granatelli built a rocket car that, according to him, reached speeds of around 180 miles per hour (290 km/h). He called the car the Firebug and toured America delighting audiences.

manufacturers asked him to do the same with their products. Baker's speed runs took him off-road. In 1914, a record-breaking transcontinental drive earned him the nickname Cannonball. This type of racing over great distances is called endurance racing.

Erwin "Cannonball" Baker set a speed and endurance record by driving from New York to Los Angeles in twelve and a half days.

TYPES OF CARS

Endurance racing requires a car with elite-level performance and reliability over long distances. For example, in the early 2000s, the Audi R8 won numerous endurance races. This particular model had an engine with 610 horsepower and a top speed of 200 miles per hour (322 km/h). Endurance races pushed carmakers to design better engines, brakes, and suspension systems.

RACES

The most glamorous endurance race is the 24 Hours of Le Mans race, held in France, which began in 1923. Drivers navigate a track—considered the best in the world—that is 8.5 miles (13.7 km) long. Unlike most races, drivers must master the dangerous task of night driving at high speeds.

The 12 Hours of Sebring race is held in Sebring, Florida. This race began in 1952. Drivers race around a track for twelve hours, and whoever is the farthest ahead wins.

WHERE TO START

Becoming a successful driver takes a lot of work, practice, and luck. Professional driver Derek Daly identified six ingredients to becoming a successful driver. They are commitment, physical skills, mental skills, communication skills, technical skills, and talent. And because cars are expensive, race car drivers also require a significant investment of money.

There are driving schools where students can learn from experienced coaches about the basics of racing in a safe, controlled environment. The schools are also a good resource for parents. Even Derek Daly's son attended racing schools that improved on his abilities.

CHAPTER TWO

TRUCKS, KARTS, AND OTHER FOUR-WHEELED RACERS

There is more to four-wheeled racing than just cars. In races like the Baja 1000, trophy trucks can reach speeds of over 135 mph (217 km/h). This is no easy feat since the trucks can weigh up to four tons. Unlike stock cars, which are built to resemble their street counterparts, Trophy trucks are designed for desert racing and most of them are not street legal. Karts are another popular option for any extreme motorsport enthusiast. These small vehicles can be raced only on closed tracks and are made of little more than an open steel frame, an engine, and wheels. Trucks and karts are only two more kinds of four-wheeled racers that extreme motorsports enthusiasts love.

MUD TRUCK RACING

For racers looking to get down and dirty, there might be nothing better than mud truck racing. As the name suggests, trucks race through sticky mud that makes it difficult for drivers to maintain control. Trucks completely stuck in the mud are a common sight.

Like other forms of racing, mud truck racing began when people met to race their cars in an open, available muddy

Mud truck racing adds an extreme environment to an already dangerous sport.

field. The awards, fans, and official races came later. Mud racing is sometimes referred to as mud bogging, and trucks are called mud boggers. These races are common at monster truck rallies. Monster trucks are pickup trucks with special engines and oversized tires.

One of the most important features for a mud truck is four-wheel drive. Four-wheel drive refers to a system that powers all four wheels at the same time. Without this system, mud trucks would have no hope of getting unstuck during a race.

Mud trucks are generally modified versions of a common truck. In addition to four-wheel drive, mud trucks have fast and powerful engines.

STADIUM SUPER TRUCK RACING

In 2012, professional race car driver Robby Gordon founded a new series of truck races. He called it the Stadium Super Trucks Series, and the new class of race has already achieved a lot of success. In 2014, the Stadium Super Trucks Series expanded its audience by joining the ESPN X Games, a major event in extreme sports, in Austin, Texas.

Just as remote-control cars are sometimes made to look like real cars, Stadium Super Trucks are made to resemble radio-control cars. The trucks are powerful, with up to six hundred horsepower engines, and can reach speeds of around 130 miles per hour (209 km/h). They are designed to race on any type of surface, but they are specifically made to jump off of ramps.

Though the races take place on courses and last around fifteen or twenty minutes, Stadium Super Truck races have many characteristics of off-road races. Trucks often bump into one another, or fly 130 feet (40 m) in the air off of one of the course ramps.

Jumping massive trucks through the air puts stress on the driver's body. Drivers have suffered everything from sore backs to broken bones from midair collisions or tumbling trucks. One driver had to do a month of physical rehabilitation to recover from a crash.

KART RACING

Kart racing can be a gateway into the bigger world of extreme motorsports. The entire family can take part in karting, while those really serious about racing can move on to more powerful vehicles. Karts are simpler versions of cars. There have no doors, windows, or even roofs. Drivers are exposed to the weather and wind while driving.

That does not mean, though, that kart racing is not meant to be taken seriously. Specific safety equipment is required in organized races, and it must meet a strict standard. Speeds can go as high as

Kart racing has become popular throughout the world. Pictured is the Asian Rotax Max Challenge in Kuala Lumpur, Malaysia.

125 miles per hour (201 km/h), which is just as fast as most cars. Kart races are run on tracks about 1,000 yards (914 m) in length. The relatively low cost of the vehicles has given the sport popular appeal.

Kart racing can trace its beginning to 1956 when a race car builder named Art Ingles built a kart out of a piece of steel tubing and a lawn mower engine. Ingles wanted a fun vehicle he could race with friends, and his passion quickly caught on.

Within a year, other people had built their own karts and it was not long after that kart racing began. The races spread beyond parking lots, and karting tracks appeared across Southern California. Large races were held throughout the 1950s and into the 1960s.

KARTING, A WHEELCHAIR-ACCESSIBLE SPORT

One of the appealing things about kart racing is that people with disabilities are able to participate. Kart designers have created vehicles that not only allow the physically challenged to participate in karting, but that put all kart racers on equal ground.

Hand-operated controls, or HOC for short, allow the driver to control speed and the brakes. Specially designed seats make the ride more comfortable for those with physical challenges. These features do not sacrifice speed, however, making all competitors truly capable of winning.

EQUIPMENT

Kart engines can be anywhere from four to fifty horsepower, although the most common engine type is twelve horsepower. Some engines use pull cords like those you see on lawn mowers, while others are electric or battery powered.

One of the most important components of a kart is the seat. Since karts are so small and light, the driver's body must be positioned correctly to ensure speed. Correct seat placement can greatly enhance speed and handling.

Safety equipment includes helmets, gloves, special shoes, rib protectors, and more. It is important to check the brakes and to ensure that all the nuts and bolts are in good condition and fastened tightly.

WHERE TO START

Racing schools are a good place to start for those interested in all kinds of racing. Attending races is another great way to learn about truck and kart racing. Talking to the drivers themselves is a way to learn specifics about the sport. Information can also be found in books, magazines, and the Internet. For example, there are magazines dedicated to karting such as *Go Racing, KartSport*, and others. Finally, doing thorough research will help when buying equipment for the first time.

CHAPTER THREE

EXTREME ON TWO WHEELS

The self-propelled bicycle appeared in Britain toward the end of the nineteenth century. It used a gasoline engine. By the turn of the century, manufacturers were converting bikes by adding small engines. Motorcycle racing in North America began in 1903.

By the end of World War I (1914–1918) motorcycle companies began to go out of business as cars became more affordable. Motorcycles were rebranded as a sport or leisure vehicle instead of day-to-day transportation. This move made sense since many people were racing their motorcycles already.

HISTORY OF MOTORCYCLE RACING

As people raced their motorcycles on the roads, promoters and racers worked on making an organized form of racing to reduce the danger they faced. Rather than risk their lives and the lives of anyone on the roads on which they raced, riders began to use tracks, as was popular in the United States, or on closed sections of public roads, as was popular in Europe.

In 1904, the European organization Fédération Internationale des Clubs Motocyclistes (FICM) was formed to oversee and

Early motorcycle races, such as this one in Essex, England, took place on dirt tracks.

promote motorcycle racing. The FICM became the Fédération Internationale de Motocyclisme (FIM) in 1949 and continues to oversee racing series around the world. In the United States, the American Motorcyclist Association (AMA) was formed in 1924. It has influence over many types of racing including motocross, enduro, supercross and others.

Motorcycles became specialized for each type of race. There are now motorcycles made for road racing, dirt-track events, off-road scrambles, freestyle, and more. Over the years, as technology improved, these motorcycle sports produced faster races and even more extreme competitions.

PUSHING MOTORCYCLE RACING TO THE EXTREME: MOTOCROSS

Many consider motocross to be the most popular style of motorcycle racing. It is a blend of motorcycling and cross-country riding. Forty riders race around a track of hills, dirt roads, sharp turns, and mud. Most races, called motos, last about thirty minutes and generally end when a racer makes a set number of laps around a track. Motocross is not meant for the beginner. It is a challenging sport that requires a lot of experience for one to succeed.

Motocross pushes both motorcycles and riders to the extreme with challenging off-road courses.

Enduro racing is similar to endurance racing for cars. These off-road trials have many different physical challenges. Some events involve time trials. Motorcycles also compete in the Baja 1000 and the Dakar Rally, a race that travels over 5,200 miles (8,369 km). Grand Prix racing refers to races that feature the most technologically

ATV MOTOCROSS

All-terrain vehicles, or ATVs, are four-wheeled versions of motorcycles. They are larger and heavier than motorcycles, but they move just as fast. Fans enjoy that ATV racers are generally closer together during a race than in other kinds of races. Because of their size, ATVs are hard to pass during a race, and experienced riders have a talent for blocking other racers behind them.

ATV motocross is gaining in popularity. However, ATV racing went through a rough patch. Many thought that ATVs were not safe for racing, and manufacturers discontinued their ATV racers. Throughout the 1980s and 1990s, people had to make their own ATV racers from the regular ATVs that remained available from manufacturers.

Today, ATV racing has its own organizations, races, and events. There are ATV races held on the same tracks and during the same events as their motorcycle motocross counterparts. One such event is called the Grand Finale, and it is held every year on country music star Loretta Lynn's ranch.

advanced motorcycles. Motorcycle Grand Prix races are very expensive to join. Leasing a championship-level bike will cost at least $1 million per season.

The United States has the AMA Motocross Championship, with dirt track and road racing. The British version is called the British Motocross Championship. There is an international event called the annual Motocross des Nations, which is sometimes called the Olympics of motocross. The event, started in 1947, is held in cities around the world. Teams from dozens of countries compete.

SUPERCROSS: GROWING BEYOND MOTOCROSS

Supercross is a style of intense racing that takes place within specialized performance off-road conditions. The turns are tighter and the tracks more demanding than other off-road races. The races are like motocross races, but the courses are inside stadiums. This came about because spectators wanted to enjoy motocross from the comfort of a stadium seat rather than outside exposed to the weather.

All obstacles are man-made, such as 6-foot (2 m) walls of dirt, series of ramped jumps, and an obstacle called a rut. This is a thin, deep groove that forms after many riders ride over the same spot. Another difference between supercross and motocross races is the presence of amateur racers. While amateur, or nonprofessional, racers can compete in motocross, only professionals can compete in supercross.

In 1974, the AMA created the AMA Supercross Series. The series is made up of sixteen separate races. These races are held between January and May of each year, and each takes place in a different city. There are strict rules so racing teams do not make unfair improvements to their motorcycles.

BIG AIR AND FREESTYLE MOTOCROSS

One of the most extreme motorsports is freestyle motocross, or FMX. Unlike motocross, there is no race. Instead, competitions are about which rider can perform the most creative and difficult tricks. In the mid-1990s, supercross racer Jeremy McGrath would perform a stunt while flying through the air and crossing the finish line. He became a favorite among fans. Race organizers created events at which other riders could perform similar tricks and FMX was born.

Freestyle motocross riders need a lot of creativity to impress the judges and the fans.

Stunts include airborne tricks like nac-nacs, which involve quick dismounts and remounts; heel-clickers, in which riders brings their heels forward over the handles and click them together; and can-cans, which involve kicking both feet in the air over one side of the bike. Riders are constantly creating newer and more daring tricks, like multiple backflips.

One variant of motocross racing is called supermoto. It combines motocross track racing with freestyle elements. A competitor rides over bumps and executes jumps while riding around a track. There are also metal ramps off of which riders can perform various tricks to show off their abilities.

Freestyle events have become more popular over time. Popular events include Red Bull X-Fighters, NIGHT of the JUMPs, and more.

WHERE TO START

Children as young as six can get into motocross. Professional riders suggest starting out by attending races. There are clubs such as the American Federation of Motorcyclists and the Central Roadracing Association. They can teach students the basics and how to become successful in the sport. They hold their own races and events.

Once a rider knows how to properly ride a motorcycle, he or she may want to become a freestyle competitor. There are ways to practice that, too. For example, FMX jumpers practice their tricks over foam pits. With the pit acting as a safety net, freestylers can experiment with new jumps and tricks.

All riders must earn a motorcycle license. Racing clubs, which sponsor amateur and professional riders, require a license to take one of their racing classes. Some racing clubs also provide discounts for students to attend a safety school.

CHAPTER FOUR

WATER, AIR, AND SNOW RACING

In 1932, Mary Haizlip became a star in a new extreme motorsport—air racing. Haizlip raced specially designed airplanes against other pilots in the Women's Shell Speed Dash, a short 2-mile (3 km) straightaway course. Spectators that day saw Haizlip set a new speed record when she reached 255 miles per hour (410 km/h). This was an amazing 45 miles per hour (72km/h) faster than the previous record.

Air racing has only grown since those early days. With water and snow motorsports also gaining more fans and participants, motorsports are hardly stuck to the ground.

29

American pilot Mary Haizlip smashed records both in speed and as a female pilot in the male-dominated sport.

AIR RACING

About six years after the Wright Brothers successfully flew the world's first airplane in 1903, the first air races took place in Rheims, France. A $10,000 prize was offered for "the best speed record by an airplane over a closed course." Since then, air racing has become an organized competitive sport.

After World War I, many pilots returned home in need of work. Some began traveling around and giving exhibitions of flying skill and performing aeronautical stunts, a practice that came to be known as barnstorming. These exhibitions included speed competitions.

A pilot performs a maneuver at a Red Bull Air Race World Championship in Sydney, Australia.

EQUIPMENT

Air racing requires an advanced level of aviation, or aircraft-related, engineering. Aerobatics pilot and champion air racer Mike Mangold explained in a 2014 interview for Fox News, "We're flying with very high G forces, at very high speeds and at very low altitudes." The G force is the amount of gravity affecting an object. The higher the G forces, the stronger an object is pulled in one direction. Flying at incredible speeds puts a large amount of force on a body and an airplane. For example, at two Gs someone who weighs 100 pounds (45 kilograms) would experience 200 pounds (91 kg) of force. This is just one factor that requires advanced airplane design for air racing.

There are four classes of air racing. They are unlimited air racing, T-6, Formula 1, and biplane. Each class features its own type of plane. Unlimited air racing features the fastest propeller-powered planes. The T-6 class features training aircraft. Formula 1 racing, on the other hand, features relatively low-cost planes that are safe to fly. A biplane is an early type of aircraft with two pairs of wings, one above the other.

Every plane has a similar engine and propeller, and planes must all weigh about the same to make sure no one gets an unfair advantage.

RED BULL AIR RACE

The Red Bull Air Race World Championship matches the world's top pilots against each other in an advanced challenge. The master class category of the championship sets twelve pilots racing through an aerial racetrack. The course is set using air-filled pylons. The point is to simply fly through the course with the fastest time.

In 2014, the Red Bull Air Race World Championship introduced the Challenger Cup. This race welcomes eleven pilots from around the world to compete and allows them to gain experience. In doing so, race organizers hope to increase safety in one of the fastest motorsports around.

EXTREME WATER SPORTS

In 1903, the owner of the British *Daily Mail* newspaper, Alfred Harmsworth, created the first annual international powerboat competition. Over time the boats became more powerful and reached ever faster speeds. Powerboat racing is considered the fastest, the most

Teams race powerful boats like this Thundercat powerboat at extreme water motorsport events.

glamorous, and most dangerous of all water sports. Boats, or vessels, reach speeds of 140 miles per hour (225 km/h).

POWERBOAT RACES

The races are categorized by boat engine size and course distance. There are both circular courses and one-way courses, also known as point-to-point. Races can be slalom style, in which drivers must perform sharp turns to follow a path of buoys. Endurance powerboat races, on the other hand, are similar to endurance car or motorcycle races.

The top class of racing boats is called Formula One or F1. Events are held around the world and attract large audiences. F1 courses are

JET SKIS

In the late 1960s, an American motorcycle rider named Clay Jacobson had an idea. Jacobson worked at a motorcycle company named Kawasaki. He made a machine that was like a motorcycle ridden on the water. This was the first Jet Ski. The Jet Ski is designed so if a rider falls off, the motor shuts off immediately.

The Jet Ski's power comes from a strong jet of water that shoots out of the back of the vehicle. Some models can reach speeds of 60 miles per hour (97 km/h). Over the years, riders have developed a large number of tricks they can perform on a Jet Ski. For example, some riders can make sharp turns, fly through the air, dive into the water, and even do somersaults.

Jet Ski racing has now become a beloved international sport.

about 6,562 feet (2,000 m) long. The boats are about 20 feet (6 m) long, and 7 feet (2 m) wide. Because the boats are designed to lift out of the water and into the air at high speeds, and F1 powerboat teams have to deal with G-forces, as pilots do, many feel that F1 racing has much in common with air racing.

DRAG BOAT RACING

Just as there is drag racing for cars, there is drag racing for boats. Similar to their car counterparts, drag boats are extremely fast. They can reach speeds of up to 230 miles per hour (370 km/h). Drag boats have large engines capable of producing an enormous amount of power. One such boat, the California Quake, had a 5,000-horse-power engine and could travel a quarter mile in under five seconds.

To reduce the boat's weight (because large, powerful engines are heavy), drag boats have only one seat, for the driver. The seat is placed inside a roll cage for extra protection and safety. Should there be a high-speed crash, the capsule holding the roll cage breaks free of the boat.

SNOWMOBILE RACING

When the weather turns cold, many extreme motorsports racers modify their vehicles for the snow and ice. In areas that receive lots of snow during the winter, snow motorsports are a popular option. Snowmobiling in particular is a competitive sport. In the 1950s, a smaller and lighter version of the snowmobile was invented. Up until then, snowmobiles were large, heavy, and used by the military, ambulances, and forest-related industries.

Snowmobiles can reach high speeds very quickly. They can hit top speeds of around 120 miles per hour (193 km/h), skimming across the ground on one or two skis in the front and with tracks

Snowmobiles provide extreme motorsport athletes a way to compete during the winter.

that look like those of military tanks toward the rear. Snowmobiles can be very noisy.

The Winter X Games feature a variety of snowmobile events, such as snocross (a race that involves tight turns, jumps, and obstacles), best trick, and best freestyle. One snowmobile jumper set a world record in 2011 by clearing a 300-foot (91 m) water gap. The freestyle events feature riders performing incredible, seemingly impossible tricks.

WHERE TO START

Getting a start in air, boat, or snowmobile racing begins with attending events. As with cars and motorcycles, earning a license to drive these vehicles is a requirement.

Because these sports take place in different environments, it is recommended that athletes learn related skills. For example, water sport participants should take swimming and scuba-diving lessons. Another tip from professionals is for learners to practice getting out of the vehicles with their eyes closed. This will be helpful in situations in which visibility is low or nonexistent.

CHAPTER FIVE

A DANGEROUS GAME

While extreme motorsports are not as popular as soccer, football, or basketball, they are growing in popularity and viewership. More new channels have given these sports coverage they would not have gotten years ago.

POPULARIZING MOTORSPORTS

One example of new television coverage for extreme motorsports is the X Games. This is an event organized by ESPN, the leader in televised sporting events. The games feature a wide variety of extreme motorsports and FMX is heavily showcased. One event, called the step-up, is like a high jump for motorcycles. There are women's and men's races and competitions. Not to be forgotten, winter sports have their own games, called the Winter X Games. There are the expected

36

Although motorsports remain dominated by male athletes, there are more and more women participating.

snowboarding and skiing events, but there are winter motorsports events, too, like snowmobile racing.

There are other televised events that have helped to popularize other extreme motorsports. The television show *Nitro Circus* brings FMX to home viewers and introduces new people to the sport. Off-road truck races are frequently aired, and drag races can be enjoyed from home, too.

TECHNICAL INNOVATIONS

In 2014 at the National Championship Air Races in Reno, a new kind of aircraft was flown: small, unmanned drones. The competition, called the Small UAS Challenge, took place over three days. Twenty private and commercial participants competed in events such as an obstacle course, a time trial, and a dead lift, in which the drones were tested for how much they could carry.

The chairman of the Reno Air Racing Association was quoted as saying, "It is a thrill for us and is something that our fans won't be able to see anywhere else in the world. This is a one-of-a-kind chance for people to get up close and personal with this technology in a fun and challenging environment."

Motorsports change over time as new technology is invented. The Small UAS Challenge is a way to promote and recognize the unmanned aerial systems industry.

DANGERS OF MOTORSPORTS

Extreme motorsports can be exciting and fun in a way that many other sports aren't. But this type of excitement comes with a risk of accident and injury. No matter if the race is on land, sea, or air, safety precautions must be taken in advance to prevent something dangerous from happening.

In 2009, freestyle motocross star Jeremy Lusk died from head injuries suffered during a crash at an event. He was attempting a backflip while making a 100-foot (30 m) jump. Lusk was unable to complete the trick and crashed into the dirt. He was able to walk away from a similar crash at the 2007 X Games, but he was not so lucky the second time. While there have been many injuries in FMX, Lusk is believed to be the first professional rider to suffer fatal injuries during competition.

Extreme motorsports can even be dangerous for the audience. Two hours into the 1955 Le Mans race, two cars collided on the track. The cars then crashed into the spectator's stand. In all, at least eighty people were killed, while another seventy-seven were injured. Incredibly, there was no official announcement of the

A year before Lusk's fatal crash he is seen here (*on the right*) carrying fellow motocross racer Blake Williams off the field after an accident.

accident and the twenty-four-hour race continued. Race organizers stated that stopping the race would have only caused alarm among the spectators and made rescue efforts difficult.

SAFETY FIRST

To avoid such accidents, professionals suggest education, enforcement, and technology. It is up to each athlete to teach himself or herself about the necessary safety precautions for each sport. Putting these lessons to use or enforcing the guidelines given by a governing body or the head of a team is the next important step. Lastly, getting suitable and working safety gear, such as a helmet, is an important component to personal safety.

Taking care to improve safety can in turn improve one's performance in these sports. It is in the best interest of athletes to take safety precautions and lower risk in order to help win races and competitions.

THE FUTURE OF EXTREME MOTORSPORTS

Racing airplanes, high-powered boats, and heavy trucks will always be dangerous. Engines will become more powerful, vehicles will be lighter, and speed records will be broken. As technology introduces new innovations to sports, safety must also follow in order to avoid tragedies like the one at the 1955 Le Mans race.

As more people are exposed to extreme motorsports, either on television or in person, the number of participating athletes will increase. In the first half of the twentieth century, women began participating in different motorsports. With women's competitions becoming a part of events such as the X Games, motorsports will have even more room to grow.

GLOSSARY

aerodynamics The study of the properties of moving air and of the interaction between the air and solid objects moving through it.

amateur A person who engages in a sport on an unpaid basis.

ATV All-terrain vehicle; a small open motor vehicle designed for use on rough ground.

component A part or element of a larger whole, especially a part of a machine or vehicle.

fjord A long, narrow, deep inlet of the sea between high cliffs.

Grand Prix Any of a series of auto-racing or motorcycling contests forming part of a world championship series, held in various countries under international rules.

horsepower The unit of power of engines equal to 550 foot-pounds per second (745.7 watts).

innovation A new method, idea, or product.

JATO Jet-assisted takeoff; an additional power unit providing extra thrust at takeoff for vehicles.

motorsport A sport involving the racing of motor vehicles, especially cars and motorcycles.

precaution A measure taken in advance to prevent something dangerous, unpleasant, or inconvenient from happening.

Prohibition The prevention by law of the manufacture and sale of alcohol in the United States between 1920 and 1933.

pylon Tall, towerlike structure.

rally raid A form of long distance off-road racing that takes place over several days.

rehabilitation Help provided for disabled or injured persons; the removal or reduction of disabilities.

rut A thin, deep groove on a race track that forms after many riders ride over the same spot.

stock car Ordinary car that has been modified for racing.

viewership The audience for a particular television program or channel.

FOR MORE INFORMATION

American Power Boat Association (APBA)
17640 East Nine Mile Road
P.O. Box 377
Eastpointe, MI 48021-0377
(586) 773-9700
Email: apbahq@apba.org
Website: http://www.apba.org
The APBA is the U.S. governing body for powerboat racing as
    authorized by the Union Internationale Motonautique.

American Youth Motorsports Team
West Palm Beach, FL 33417
(772) 285-7208
Website: http://www.aymt.org
The American Youth Motorsports Team, Inc., incorporates
    motorsports to teach girls and boys between the ages of six and
    eighteen about abuse of alcohol, tobacco, and street crime.

Bridgestone Racing Academy
Box 373
Pontypool, ON L0A 1K0
Canada
(905) 983-1114
Website: https://www.race2000.com
The Bridgestone Racing Academy teaches drivers of all levels and can
    help students earn their licenses.

International Snowmobile Racing, Inc.
1527 N Railroad Street
Eagle River, WI 54521
(262) 335-2401
Website: http://www.isrracing.org

The International Snowmobile Racing, Inc., is a service organization established to provide for the needs of individual clubs and organizations that conduct snowmobile races.

MSI Youth Foundation
2509 North Delaware Street
Indianapolis, IN 46205
(317) 920-9500
Website: http://msiyf.org
The MSI Youth Foundation teaches young people about leadership values and healthy living through sports.

Reno Air Racing Association
14501 Mount Anderson Street
Reno, NV 89506
(775) 972-6663
Website: http://airrace.org
The Reno Air Racing Association organizes one of the biggest air racing events in the United States.

WEBSITES

Because of the changing nature of Internet links, Rosen Publishing has developed an online list of websites related to the subject of this book. This site is updated regularly. Please use this link to access this list:

http://www.rosenlinks.com/STTE/Motor

FOR FURTHER READING

Adamson, Thomas K. *Dirt Bike World: Motocross Racing*. North Mankato, MN: Capstone Press, 2010.

David, Jack. *Supercross Racing*. Minneapolis, MN: Bellwether Media, 2009.

Evans, Sheila, Jennifer Gough, and Sally Paxton. *Motor Sports*. Clayton South, Victoria, Australia: Blake Education, 2010.

Gifford, Clive. *The Inside Story of Motorsports*. New York, NY: Rosen Publishing, 2011.

Gifford, Clive. *Karting*. London, England: Franklin Watts, 2009.

Kelley, K. C. *Drag Racing*. Tarrytown, NY: Marshall Cavendish Benchmark, 2010.

MacLean, Glynne. *Extreme Acceleration*. Auckland, New Zealand: Pearson, 2012.

Roselius, J. Chris. *Danica Patrick: Racing to History*. Berkeley Heights, NJ: Enslow Publishers, 2009.

Spalding, Lee. *Off-Road Racing*. Vero Beach, FL: Rourke Publishing, 2009.

BIBLIOGRAPHY

BBC. "On This Day June 11 1955: Le Mans disaster claims 77 lives." BBC News. Retrieved September 28, 2014.

Buckley, James. *Scholastic Year in Sports 2012*. New York, NY: Scholastic, 2011.

Cavin, Curt. "Robby Gordon's Stadium Super Truck Series exciting for fans." *Autoweek*, May 19, 2014.

Cooper, Ann L. *Stars of the Sky, Legends All: Illustrated Histories of Women Aviation Pioneers*. St. Paul, MN: Zenith Press, 2008.

Daly, Derek, and Mario Andretti. *Race to Win: How to Become a Complete Champion Driver*. St. Paul, MN: MBI Pub. Co. LLC and Motorbooks, 2008.

Ellison, Betty Boles. *Early Laps of Stock Car Racing: A History of the Sport and Business Through 1974*. Jefferson, NC: McFarland & Company, Inc., Publishers, 2014.

Gelston, Dan. "Austin Dillon wins on Dirt at Eldora." *AP Sports Auto Racing*, July, 25 2013.

Gigliotti, Jim. *Off-Road Racing*. New York, NY: Marshall Cavendish Benchmark, 2010.

Heckler, Ike. *Drag Racing 101: From Building Your First Race Car to Securing Sponsors*. CreateSpace Independent Publishing Platform, 2010.

Howell, Brian. *Mud Truck Racing: Tearing It Up*. Minneapolis, MN: Lerner Publishing Group, 2014.

Lerner, Preston, and Matthew L. Stone. *History's Greatest Automotive Mysteries, Myths, and Rumors Revealed: James Dean's Killer Porsche, NASCAR's Fastest Monkey, Bonnie and Clyde's Getaway Car, and More*. Minneapolis, MN: Motorbooks, 2012.

Markham, Derek. "Top 6 Most Extreme Motorsports." *DNews*, November 22, 2011.

McCollum, Sean. *Sports Cars*. Mankato, MN: Capstone Press, 2010.

Molloy, Fran. Extreme: *Jobs Your Mother Doesn't Want You to Know*

About. Australia. Ultimo, New South Wales, Australia: Career FAQs, 2006.

Olson, Jeff. "Le Mans Death Reminder of 'Dangerous Sport' Say Drivers." *USA Today*, June 22, 2013.

O'Neil, Devon. "Racing's Best-Kept Secret: Super Trucks." ESPN, June 19, 2014. Retrieved October 12, 2014.

Palermo, Elizabeth. "Whoosh! Air Race Showcases Extreme Engineering." *Fox News*, September 6, 2014.

Parker, Steve. Boat-Mania! Milwaukee, WI: Gareth Stevens, 2004.

Red Bull Air Race. "About Red Bull Air Race."

Sewell, Tes. "South Africa Makes a Fitting Finale for X-Fighters." ESPN, September 3, 2014.

Shei, Tim. *Supercross Racing*. Mankato, MN: Capstone Press, 2006.

Short, Brandon. "MX: Redemption Bid Falls Just Short for Team USA at Motocross of Nations." *SPEED: The Motors On FOX Blog*, October 4, 2013. Retrieved October 16, 2014.

Speed Energy Formula Off-Road Presented by Traxxas. "About." 2014. Retrieved October 12, 2014 (http://stadiumsupertrucks.com/ssts/about).

Stealey, Bryan. *Motorcross*. New York, NY: Marshall Cavendish Benchmark, 2010.

Summers, David, and Tarda Davison-Aitkins. *The Sports Book: The Sports, the Rules, the Tactics, the Techniques*. New York, NY: Penguin, 2013.

Thomas, Pete. "Jeremy Lusk dies at 24; freestyle motocross star." *Los Angeles Times*, February 11, 2009.

Wartinger, Bob. *A Driver's Guide to Safe Boat Racing*. Raleigh, NC: Lulu Enterprises, 2008.

Yamaha Racing. "What Is MXGP?" Retrieved October 16, 2014 (http://www.yamaha-racing.com/Racing/mxgp/what_is).

INDEX

ABOUT THE AUTHOR

Jeff Mapua is a graduate of the University of Texas at Austin. He writes for students of all ages. Mapua was thrilled to take part in off-road truck racing in Nevada. Getting a chance to meet the racers and even take a lap around the track will be a favorite memory. He comes from a family of motorsports athletes, including his motorcycle-racing father. Mapua lives in Dallas, Texas, with his wife, Ruby.

PHOTO CREDITS